THE DEVIL HAS BLUE EYES

A. BADMAN

The Devil Has Blue Eyes
Copyright © 2024 by A. Badman.

All rights reserved. No part of this publication may be reproduced, distributed, or transmitted in any form or by any means, including photocopying, recording, or other electronic or mechanical methods, without the written consent of the publisher. The only exceptions are for brief quotations included in critical reviews and other non-commercial uses permitted by copyright law.

MILTON & HUGO L.L.C.
4407 Park Ave., Suite 5
Union City, NJ 07087, USA

Website: *www. miltonandhugo.com*
Hotline: *1- 888-778-0033*
Email: *info@miltonandhugo.com*

Ordering Information:
Quantity sales. Special discounts are granted to corporations, associations, and other organizations. For more information on these discounts, please reach out to the publisher using the contact information provided above.

Library of Congress Control Number:	2024904756	
ISBN-13:	979-8-89285-141-1	[Paperback Edition]
	979-8-89285-253-1	[Hardback Edition]
	979-8-89285-142-8	[Digital Edition]

Rev. date: 05/22/2024

This is book is dedicated to my two wonderful children. They have absolutely no idea how much strength they have given me and they are my "reason". Even in the worst of times, I will always fight to make sure they have a good life, and they will never have to suffer the consequences of a bad man. Everything I do is simply for them, and they have made a bigger impact on my life than anyone ever could. I love you both so much.

CONTENTS

Chapter One
The Beginning 1

Chapter Two
The Fairytale 5

Chapter Three
The Unraveling 15

Chapter Four
Lies and More Lies 25

Chapter Five
When Does It End 35

Chapter Six
Can't Run from the Truth 41

Chapter Seven
Victims 51

Chapter Eight
Facing Reality 59

About the Author 67

Flowers are often bought in times of happiness and also in moments of grief. They are given to someone to bring a smile to their face and make them feel better. Each flower has a different meaning that can represent several emotional states.

Flowers symbolize so many things for me because I was given flowers by this person for every little occasion. Sometimes there was no occasion, but he gave them to me anyway, to feel like the luckiest girl in the world. I thought it would be appropriate to start each chapter with a flower that symbolizes how everything unfolded and the way each flower represented every emotion I felt in that specific chapter. Keep in mind that these are my interpretations of these flowers and how they relate to me.

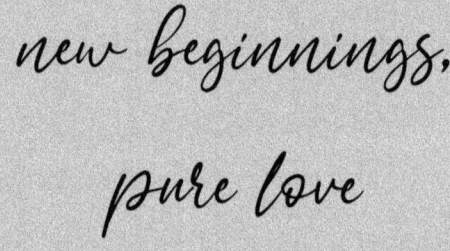

new beginnings,

pure love

CHAPTER ONE
The Beginning

Have you ever thought that you would be stuck working a normal job and everything in your life would just be another replication of each day? Typically, having the early work schedule consisted of waking up before the sun rose, getting ready for work, going to work and dealing with the stresses of whatever conflicts arose that day, coming home to make sure everything was done, and then repeating it all over again. At this point, it seems like you are just surviving and doing what needs to be done to get by and pay your bills, living paycheck to paycheck. Never in any given moment would you think that one day, you would be working remotely because of COVID, and find yourself on a dating app during one of your breaks and swiping and within a few minutes connecting to someone who seemed too good to be true. Now this person stood out because he said all the right things, he related to every little thing you could possibly have to talk about. Talk about a knight in shining armor! Typically, with my online dating experience, I would choose to talk to someone for at least a week before meeting up with them, simply because I wanted to make sure they were worth my time. On the other hand, when I currently had a guy on the other side of the phone telling me exactly what I wanted to hear, why not meet him that same night to make sure he is who he says he is?

Chapter One

On June 30, 2021, my life forever changed. As I type that sentence out, no one would possibly have any idea of what would happen in the next two and a half years to come. We all hear crazy dating stories that we can laugh about or stories that warn us of the red flags to look out for, but let me tell you, I never saw my story playing out like this. I never in my lifetime imagined going through all of this, in fact, going through something that I would be able to write a book about. Even going through something that I would want the entire world to know about because not a lot of people can relate to anything close to what this one man has put me through. I have enough memories from the past two and a half years that would make anyone go crazy. But, instead of going crazy, I find it easier to sit down and write about the events that I experienced and hopefully never have to relive them after this.

On that day in June, the day we started talking, plans were made to take place after I had gotten off of work. I was so hopeful after texting back and forth, so I decided to move forward with meeting this particular guy, who shall remain unnamed for now and the rest of this story. We decided to meet at a bar at Disney Springs, because what better place could we have chosen to sit down and get to know each other? As time went by and it was time to meet him, I was so nervous, I didn't know how this was going to go and if it would be awkward for either of us. I remember sitting in the parking lot talking to my friend on the phone, asking for reassurance to get me through the anxiety I was facing. This was so out of the norm for me, but I told myself I had nothing to lose.

Upon meeting him, he was smiling nonstop, charming, and everything you would want when meeting someone for the first time. We sat down at the bar that night and talked endlessly. There were so many laughs and stories and it kept on going until we lost track of time. When I think of this moment, it feels like something straight out of a movie. Eventually, the bartender had to hint to us that they were about to be closed, but we could take our drinks to

The Beginning

go. People were coming and going in the background whom we didn't even notice because we were so busy getting to know each other. That's when we knew the date had been so incredible that we didn't even realize we talked for as long as we did. At least to me, it felt like that.

Looking back at that day now, some people are natural charmers because they have hidden intentions. They can hide everything with a smile and tell you stories that you can relate to on every level. Just thinking about that day, I cannot believe I was able to let someone reel me in so soon and that easily. After meeting someone one time, I was able to let myself be vulnerable, thinking I found happiness and someone I could share so many stories with.

After we said goodbye that night, it wasn't long before we met again. We talked all day and every day, simply about everything there was to talk about, life, past experiences, and current issues we were facing. Heck, I didn't even know I was a person who could talk to someone as much as I talked to him. Whenever I opened up about something, I received a response and acknowledgment from him and he seemed to care more than anyone in the world. Looking back, I never thought I would be sitting here knowing that every single thing I shared, he would, in turn, use against me a few years later.

love,

beauty,

luxury

CHAPTER TWO
The Fairytale

During this time, it was 2021 and we were in the middle of the pandemic, so I was forced to live in an Airbnb while my home was being built. I was working from home, and to my surprise, this man after a week of knowing him, was showing up every single night to spend time with me and bring me dinner. He would make small gestures, such as bringing me flowers and running away before I got to the door, so it felt like a surprise. I remember one particular day, he texted me and told me to go to my front door, and to my surprise, I saw this beautiful flower arrangement. At that moment, my heart melted because there are not a lot of people who do things like that, especially on a random day, and for no specific occasion. Later on, he told me he called his florist and had them make that arrangement with my favorite colors just for me. How romantic, right?

We were going out on so many dates, and having so many dinners together, we were the absolute perfect match, and to think this all started on a random day while swiping on the Bumble dating app. What could possibly go wrong? I met my prince charming. I met the guy who I could see a future with, and the one who I felt I could have kids with and love forever. We had spontaneous days at The Melting Pot, where we would show up and he would have a table ready with candles and rose petals.

Chapter Two

The servers would ask if we were celebrating anything special and he would say, "Just another Tuesday", to make it seem like this happened all the time. Oh, how many "just another Tuesdays" we had.

Within the first few months of meeting, he had explained to me that he had spent most of his summer that year in Mexico, as he owned a home there. When we were getting to know each other, he mentioned that he traveled a lot and in fact, he was leasing a home not too far from where my Airbnb was. There were times when he said he had to go and spend time with his family, so he would occasionally leave for the day. Other than that, he spent every night with me, making sure I had food and was staying with me to make sure I wasn't alone. He even told me his chef could make meals for me because I wanted to try to be healthy instead of going out to eat all the time.

There were times when he would tell me random things about his past, which I never really paid much mind to because everyone has a past. One time, he specifically felt the need to point out that his friends often referred to him as Dan Bilzerian because years ago he would do crazy things, like rent yachts and have a lot of women follow him around because he had a lot of money. This in itself should've been a red flag, but naïve me didn't think anything of it. He also told me he was looking for several different outlets to make money, and he was even starting a vodka business. He said after they were done testing the vodka, we could fly to the distillery to try it out. Around this time, he also said he owned a recording studio and was stressed out by everything the job entailed. On some days while I worked from home, he said he was going to his studio and would be back after work. He was always supportive in every way, and always made sure he was there for me after work.

After staying at my first Airbnb for a year, the lease was about to be up, and it was time for me to move again because my home was not finished being built. To my surprise, I found another Airbnb right next to the one I was staying at. I remember being stressed out during this time because there was a lot to move and I felt like I didn't have a lot of help, even if the Airbnb was right next door. Again, my knight in shining armor was there to help me move everything over! He made the effort and showed true dedication to make sure I didn't stress myself out when it came time to move. I was the luckiest girl in the world, and I told myself this many times, even in the years to come.

After a few weeks of meeting, and spending almost every waking day together, the person who remains unnamed, had a birthday coming up. He had mentioned that he wanted to spend his birthday in Vegas, but all of his friends were too busy. I distinctly remember him reaching out to me, given we had only been together for about two months at this time, and he asked me to go with him. A trip to Vegas? What a once in a lifetime opportunity! Of course, I said yes! Who wouldn't want to go to Vegas and spend quality time with the person of their dreams?

I remember flying there and seeing the view from the plane, it was all so amazing. Let me not forget to mention, that most of the times we traveled, we were in the Delta Sky Lounge, and we also traveled first class quite a bit. This was something I was not used to or ever thought I would get to experience. I took in every single moment and never took it for granted. When we landed in Vegas, to my surprise, there was a limo waiting to pick us up. We were getting attention from people driving on the road, who were taking pictures of the limo. I remember laughing because these people had no idea who we were, but probably assumed that someone "of importance" must have been in that limo, because who randomly gets a limo to show up at a resort? When we showed up at the Caesars Palace, everyone was looking at us because we were getting out of a limo, little did they know, we were simply "no one".

Chapter Two

The feeling I got while walking into the Cesar Palace was something straight out of the scene of a movie. I was wined and dined and we spent all night at the casinos and watching shows. We did everything there was to do in Vegas, like I said, straight out of a movie. What a dream vacation it was, and it happened shortly after meeting the man of my dreams. After returning home from that vacation, I spent a total of three months in the second Airbnb until my home was finally ready to be moved into. I talked with this person because it was time to move again. He told me he had a realtor working with him and he was purchasing land in the area. He had a blueprint of the three-million-dollar house he wanted to build and all he needed was the land for it. He even showed me a contract that he signed.

Although it was extremely odd, he came crying to me one day and told me that he misread the contract and instead of putting twenty percent down, they took out way more than that, which was almost all the money he had in his bank account. He said he didn't know how he was going to pay the bills until he figured out how to get his money back. I was so concerned because I could see how unhappy he was about this, so I asked if there was anything I could do to help. He told me if I sent him fifteen hundred dollars, then it would be enough to cover his bills for that month because everything else had previously been paid for. Looking back, how would a "millionaire" only need fifteen hundred dollars to cover his bills? All the red flags were there, but they went unnoticed because I was so in love!

After that situation seemed to sort itself out, we discussed the possibility of moving in together because we spent every waking day together, so why not? He told me he put his plans to build his three-million-dollar home on pause because he wanted to move in with me. Also, what a coincidence, he told me his lease was about to be up for the current home he was staying in, so it was the perfect time for him to move in with me. He also told me that

The Fairytale

he brought the idea up to his mom and she was fully supportive of him. How convenient because I brought the idea up to mine as well, and she said she had never seen me this happy, so why not give it a shot?

It was around October 2021 when we started moving everything into my new home. I couldn't be more excited about this outcome. I had this new home that I worked so hard to buy, I was able to provide for my son, and all in the meantime, have the person who I was falling in love with move in with me. What could possibly go wrong? The only red flag around moving time was that he showed up with three storage bins full of his stuff. I asked what happened to everything else since he previously told me that he had boxes everywhere in the house that he was leasing, which was his reason for never letting me go to that home. He told me he had a storage unit where he was keeping all of his other belongings that he didn't need to move, so they would remain there in the meantime.

After we got settled in, we came up with a new schedule for my son that included dropping him off at his dad's and grandparents' house. On the days that we had my son, we would walk to the park, ride scooters, and play tag in the playground. This person spent quality time with my son to fill the "void" of his dad always being at work. There was even one day when he rented a shaved ice truck to surprise him and make him feel special. I'll never forget the smile and excitement on my sons' face, in fact, I took many pictures that day to remember the exact moment. We were so involved to the point that he was purchasing designer clothes for my son to wear to school, to make sure he was always looking his best, meanwhile, secretly promoting that he had money. We went on with our routine in this home for several months.

There were many occasions when we took the time to travel and make memories together. We went to Boston, Utah, Hawaii, St. Louis, Tennessee, and it seemed as if the traveling was endless!

Chapter Two

This wasn't normal traveling either, because we were staying at luxurious places and being treated like royalty. On many Vegas trips, he would tip our drivers a hundred dollars for only driving us a few miles. I remember when our luggage guy took our two suitcases up to our room and he got a hundred-dollar tip. I guess I never understood the point of all of it, except to flash that he had a ton of money. I could write about each individual trip and how luxurious everything was, but that would defeat the purpose of this book, and I honestly don't care to relive those memories, as they were all a fake fairy tale.

We lived pretty amazing lives, however, some questions were raised and ignored during this time. He had previously mentioned to me that he had a Lamborghini and he didn't tell a lot of people about it because he didn't want people to "use" him in any way after they found out he had money. This was the reason he never brought his fancy car around me, he said he wanted me to like him for him, which it already was a given that I did. I never understood why he couldn't just show me once so I wouldn't have to question him again. The way I felt about him overpowered my concerns and I just accepted the fact that he wasn't ready to show me the car.

When we moved into the home, I remember getting in a fight with my sister because she said if he actually owned that type of car, why would he hide it from me? At that time, I should have looked more into these concerns, but in my head, I was in this for love, not some stupid car. A few weeks after we moved into the home, he decided to tell me he was bringing home a McLaren that he just bought. He explained that the Lamborghini he had was getting high on mileage so he decided to sell it for a McLaren. Even though I asked to see the Lamborghini just one time, he told me he didn't want me to because it held a lot of memories with his ex-wife, so I let the situation go. After he got the McLaren and drove it up to the house, the look on my sons' face was priceless. The look on a lot of people's faces was priceless. He took my son

The Fairytale

for a test drive in the car and I remember recording every moment of it. It was a very cool car, but at the end of the day, the car didn't matter, the way he treated me mattered.

After a few months had gone by, he walked through the front door saying he had a surprise for me. He told me he bought me a gift because "I deserved it", and proceeded to pull out a Gucci box with a headband in it. I was excited, as it was the first designer thing I had ever gotten, and I definitely would never spend so much money on myself. I guess you could say the fancy car and the Gucci headband were the start of MANY lies to come, in the months and years to come.

Christmas 2021 came around and I was showered in designer presents. For my birthday, I was showered with diamonds. For Valentine's Day, I walked down the stairs that had hundreds of rose petals, and once I got downstairs, there were candles and balloons everywhere. This was the most romantic gesture anyone had ever given me, especially for our first Valentine's Day together. I was not only being treated right but he was giving me love and affection, and also buying me these things I didn't ask for to try and make me feel special. Who does this? This HAS to be too good to be true. But it kept on going on like this for as long as I could remember. Another thing that stood out about this man was that he was a huge family man. For every holiday, we would get matching t-shirts and spend it with his family. Everyone was so nice and accepting and the feelings were just genuine. It's one thing to meet someone who exceeds your expectations, but when his family does so as well, that's an entirely different story.

During our time living in the home, he said that he had gotten a buyer who approached him several times about selling his recording studio. He said this buyer had approached him before but now he was seriously considering it because he was sick of all of the driving back and forth and the offer was a little too good to refuse. I remember the day he came home with the news that he

Chapter Two

had decided to sell the recording studio for four million dollars. How amazing was this! I was so supportive and happy for him. He didn't have to worry about driving back and forth, plus he made a great profit when he wasn't even considering selling.

The days went by, and we discussed our plans for the future. We decided we wanted to have a baby together because life was seemingly perfect. We wanted my son to go to a better school than the one he was attending at the time. I also wanted to find a home that was closer to my job, as I was driving over 70 miles a day roundtrip. Since COVID wasn't much of a thing anymore, I was able to work in the office again. I kept looking for homes in better areas where the traffic wouldn't be as crazy as it was where we were currently living. As I came across these homes, I presented them to him. The houses were either a complete hit or miss.

One day, I came across the most beautiful house for rent. I remember showing it to him and he said he was amazed by the house too. We looked at the pictures together and saw this as a place we could grow together. We just HAD to reach out to the property manager and get a showing as soon as possible! I applied for the showing, and he did as well, just so we could increase our chances of getting a callback. Within a few days, we got the call we were waiting for and they agreed to show us the home. I was screaming with excitement because, in my head, this home had every single thing I had ever wanted for my family.

When we went to the showing, we walked in and it was truly a dream come true. Each room was perfect, each wall was perfect, and the pool was perfect! This home wasn't the average home either, it had an apartment attached to it, as well as an entirely separate room that could be used for something like a gym. One could only ever wish to live in such a magnificent home. After the showing, we talked about the house the entire way home and both decided we wanted to get an application in as soon as possible. The rental manager mentioned that they were only doing showings

The Fairytale

that weekend, as the home had a lot of interested renters and they didn't want there to be a high traffic of people coming in and out.

I remember sitting at work, talking to him, asking for updates daily until one day I received the phone call saying we got the house! How lucky were we? Out of everyone who applied for that home, by some miracle, they chose us. I was at work, sitting in my cubicle with tears in my eyes. How could life be so perfect? I was going to have a home where my son would be in a better school. I was going to be closer to work, and I would wake up every day in this house that was simply amazing. This house truly meant a new life for me and I always thought this was the beginning of many new opportunities. This was also a fresh start from my past, from everything I had to endure that remained covered. There aren't a lot of people who know what I've been through in this lifetime, but this house was just a new way to start over, forget about the past, and look forward to the future.

purity and falsehood

CHAPTER THREE

The Unraveling

When it was time to move into the home, he made a deal with the owners saying he would pay the first 6 months' rent upfront. The rent alone for this house was $7,000.00 a month, but for someone who says he makes hundreds and thousands of dollars a month from doing foreign exchange trading, this wouldn't even put a dent in his pocket. There was no worry in my mind that things wouldn't work out, and I based this on what he had told me and the actions he'd shown the last few months prior to getting this home.

On June 22, 2022, when it came time to pay the cost of getting into the house, he said that the rental manager had a system that wouldn't let him use his bank account to make that large payment, so we had to think of other options because there was no way we weren't going to get that house. I asked him about credit cards and he said that was an acceptable form of payment but his limits weren't very high because he used cash for everything. This was convenient for him because I had excellent credit and a ton of credit cards with no balances.

We scrambled around the house to gather all my credit cards to see if the limits would be enough to use to pay for the first 6 months' rent to get into this house. I found 7 of my credit cards, and we maxed them out with the agreement that he would use

Chapter Three

his bank account to pay them all off before the first billing cycle hit. Again, why would I even doubt that he wouldn't pay off the balances when he had a McLaren and paid for us to go to dinner weekly, and we had taken so many trips together? After all my cards were processed, we were finally able to move into the new home a week later. Let me just tell you, I had no idea what the future held!

By July 1, 2022, we moved into this amazing home and we were about to start a whole new chapter of our lives. I ended up selling my home and made a seventy-thousand-dollar profit, which I gave to him to "invest" because he assured me that this money would make me so much more money. I had no doubt in my mind, seeing as life was seemingly perfect and things were progressing in such an ideal way. My job at the time was very stressful and I had been at that place for about 9 years, and the field itself was stressful. He mentioned that maybe I should quit my job and he would provide since he was so successful with his trading and would be able to invest my money. The day came about two weeks after moving into the new house when I put all of my faith and trust in him. I said I had enough of the job and if he could make me money, then I would put my two weeks in. He was all on board for that, and completely supportive. At that time, we had also been trying for months to have a baby, but we weren't having any luck. I figured things would eventually align and everything would be okay.

At the beginning of August 2022, I put my two weeks' notice in, which was bittersweet for me. It felt as if I was leaving a part of myself behind, and my family as well. I had high hopes for the future. I found that I had another forty thousand dollars invested in my 401k that I decided to cash out early because he told me his accountant could do something with my taxes so there would be no penalty for withdrawing the money early. In total, I gave him one hundred and ten thousand dollars to invest in his trading,

The Unraveling

which he was so willing to do because he claimed that he loved me and we were a team. Keep in mind, I was still completely maxed out on my cards because he kept on making excuses as to why he had not been able to pay them. In his eyes, it was never his fault for not paying them, there was also an excuse with the banks and issues with their transfers. He also found reasons for every single situation. But, I continued to ignore the red flags.

A week after putting my two weeks' notice in, I found out I was pregnant! It seemed like the timing had lined up perfectly for us. We had moved into this amazing house, I put my two weeks in, and now I was pregnant and I was going to be staying at home with no stress for the months to come. On one of my last days at work, I sat in my car and made a video about how happy I was to be pregnant. I had tears in my eyes because after several months of trying, the moment was finally here. I seriously didn't think the timeline could've matched up any better. When I told him the news, he was overjoyed and many tears were shed. This was finally our time to have a baby and our dreams were becoming reality. We had a new home to live in, a new schedule and routine with my son and his school, and now we were going to have a little family of our own.

The feeling at that time was indescribable, as I had so many emotions because I just kept thinking to myself how life couldn't be any better than it was at that exact moment. Everything I had ever hoped and wished for, was right there in front of me and there was no turning back. On the last day of my job, I said my goodbyes and it was very sad for me to pack my stuff up and leave. It was difficult to not reminisce on all the opportunities and friendships I had spent 9 years building, but I knew everything happened for a reason. This reason, however, was not the reason I had hoped for, and you will find out exactly why as the story continues.

Chapter Three

After I left my job, we stayed busy by going on dates and just spending time with each other. We had annual passes to Sea World, Disney, and Universal, so there was a lot for us to do and we made the most of it. There was one night when we went to SeaWorld and I remember getting a friend request from his ex-wife. I showed it to him and he immediately told me to block her. I thought his reaction was a bit off, but he said he didn't know why she would even try to add me, but he didn't want her telling me any lies. Of course, I had nothing else to go by, so as requested, I immediately blocked her. Later, it would come to light that there was a reason she tried adding me and if I hadn't told him, my future could have been saved in that one short interaction.

As we got settled into the new house, having the thought of a life growing inside of me was simply amazing and we were more in love than ever. We were getting adjusted to this new routine of being home together and figuring out what our future would be like. He was busy swooning me with his thoughtfulness and giving my son more attention than he could ever ask for. He taught my son how to ride a bike, ice skate, ride a scooter, and he even signed him up for baseball! Many nights at the new home were spent upstairs playing video games and just enjoying each other's company. Everyone seemed to be happy, my son most of all, was happy with his new life. Every holiday that passed, I would decorate and host get-togethers for his family, and it was always talked about. We would celebrate every little occasion and never took a single second of us being together for granted.

Not only was our life as a little family perfect, but in the background, he said he was making tons of money for both of us. When he said this, it always put my mind at ease because I knew I didn't quit my job for nothing. I was able to have a family and spend quality time with them, all while making money to support my future. Or so I thought.

The Unraveling

Every time he said he traded, he would send me screenshots of the profit he made. Sometimes, he had days where he made ten thousand dollars and other days it was over one hundred fifty thousand dollars! I would write every single trade down and I even made an Excel spreadsheet so I could keep up with all the profit I was making. A few short months after leaving my job, I remember texting him saying "I'm officially a millionaire". His trading was doing so well that the profit he made for me put me at a million dollars in less than half a year! At this time, I was asking him to send me wires since I was making so much profit, and he would tell me that his banks were having issues, or making mistakes and that's why the wires weren't going through. I didn't think anything of it, because I was a "millionaire", and he told me the more money you have, the more issues you will have getting your money out.

It had been a year since he promised to pay my credit cards off. I was growing weary because I was accruing more interest than I could even fathom. My credit scores were being impacted severely, but he kept reassuring me that they were going to get paid off eventually. There were times that I would just sit down and cry because I had worked so hard to get to where I was, and now my cards were maxed out and I could only trust his word that he was going to pay them off. The only thing I had to go by to know I had money were the spreadsheets I made because he kept making up different reasons as to why the profit I was asking for wasn't hitting my bank account.

In December 2022, there was one particular day that he was acting extra weird. I already knew what was coming because it was something we had talked about for months. He told me to get dressed up, so I did the best that I could being five months pregnant at the time. He made me put on a blindfold and took me to a warehouse where he said he had an entire set built for me. I had tears in my eyes at the time because I knew exactly what was happening. As he took me out of the car, I had to keep my blindfold on and he was taking me in one room at a time and I was able to take the blindfold off to see the setup. He did this until I was able to see every room. He recreated our entire relationship in a set of rooms, and at the end of it got down on one knee and asked me to marry him. I remember him saying that we had done everything together and he simply couldn't imagine doing it with anyone else. As he opened the ring box, there was a huge diamond inside, which he later went on to tell me that he spent over one hundred thousand dollars on for that ring. He also said it took months to build that set for me, but he had been planning the proposal for about five months. We went and celebrated our engagement at dinner after that. Talk about living in a dream!

During half the year 2022 and well into 2023, he was buying Lamborghini's and more fancy cars than you would see in the parking lot of a car dealership. He even bought me a Lamborghini Huracan and Lamborghini Urus, simply because I "deserved" it. Even though he was purchasing all of these expensive things, that he constantly showed off on social media, he still kept coming up with excuses as to why he couldn't pay off my cards. For about a year, he told me that he was waiting for the rental manager to refund my cards and they weren't doing it for some odd reason. The excuses were endless when it came to sending my wires and paying off my cards, but when it came time to purchase luxurious things and post them on social media, he always found a way to make that happen. At one point, he said he had two Lamborghini Huracáns, two Lamborghini Urus', a Ferrari, a McLaren, and a Rolls Royce. Of course, we only had one or two of these cars in our garage at the time because he kept all of the others in his "second garage".

All of his "success" and the posts he was making on social media would bring the attention of a lot of people. I knew several people, who shall remain unnamed, who decided to go ahead and "invest" with him. One person alone, invested over two hundred and fifty thousand dollars because they were reassured that he could make them a ton of profit by trading. Everyone wanted a little bit of success and if someone was more than willing to help them, then why not invest as well? He promoted his success by posting videos on social media saying he wanted to give back to the community and would choose to pay random people's rent if they were struggling. He wanted to give back, yet he couldn't pay off the debt he put his fiancé in at the time!

We had random days where we would meet at Gucci and he would spend twenty-five thousand dollars on items for his family and me, and it was "just because" he could. Again, I was still maxed out in debt and would cry every week because my credit cards weren't getting paid off. For our gender reveal in February 2023, he made sure he got several celebrities to be a part of our reveal video, telling us their guesses on what the gender of our baby was going to be. It was magical. He told me he had a connection who personally reached out to these celebrities for the videos. As I reflect on those videos, it was more of him paying for them to make a cameo versus him having a "connect". He even said his connect got Post Malone to agree to perform at our wedding and when he was approached by the connect, he said Post Malone's response was "I've never been invited to a wedding before". Reading all these words just makes me want to bang my head against the wall because all of these situations seem so ridiculous now, but in hindsight, I was fully taken back and believed everything.

For Valentine's Day that year, I was about seven months pregnant and he made it EXTRA special by getting a private jet to take us to Miami and we spent the entire day on a yacht. He made sure to tell me that day cost him over eighty thousand dollars. The private jet had rose petals everywhere. The yacht had balloons and rose petals everywhere. This was one of the most romantic gestures I had ever experienced in my life. We had lunch on the back of the

Chapter Three

yacht while we were served by a private staff that was hired just for us for the day. That was truly a day I would never forget.

Throughout my entire pregnancy, he would take his family and friends on Disney and Universal VIP tours. Mind you, each of these tours cost about ten thousand dollars, and I would say we went on at least six of them. The world looked at our social media wishing they could do these extravagant things. My friends and family told me over and over how lucky I was to find such an amazing man who not only did these things for me but also showed me how much he loved me emotionally. They all said they were so happy I was bringing a baby into this world because she would forever be lucky and cherished by everyone, especially him.

We ended up going on the Disney Wish cruise and South Carolina before my baby girl was born. We even sat courtside at the Magic game in Orlando! These were the last moments we had together before our family grew bigger, so it was special that we had these times alone. The time came for my girl to make her entrance into the world. I was thirty-nine weeks pregnant and in triage for about fifteen hours. He was losing his patience so much that he punched the wall. As I was confined to the bed the entire time, I remember him bickering back and forth with the nurse who kept walking in to check on me. When I was finally moved into the delivery room, I was in labor for over another fifteen hours. The entire time I was so uncomfortable and screaming in pain towards the end, as I didn't have an epidural, but I remember I was more worried about his well-being and making sure he was okay instead of worrying about myself. This just goes to show how much one person can control you mentally, that you would put them first, even when you're in such a critical situation, such as childbirth. Baby girl was born the day before my birthday and I'll never forget that moment where I got to hold her. My family was complete. Life was amazing and it couldn't get any better at that exact moment. Boy, was I wrong.

The Unraveling

I ignored little things in my life, like the anger issues he had. If anyone crossed him, he said he knew people who could go after them and "take care of them". The day I was in labor, he punched the wall because the nurses were taking too long to get me a room. If something didn't go his way, it was the end of the world and I had to deal with the emotional stages of him. If something was an issue, I had to do something to correct it, otherwise I would never hear the end of it. When he had a question about something, he always had to call his parents for reassurance. You see, the process of falling in love sometimes includes avoiding all of these red flags, and oh MY, were there so many red flags.

After I spent over thirty hours in labor, I had to give him my hospital bed because he complained about how uncomfortable he was with sleeping on the pull-out bed. All these little things seemed okay in the moment because it felt like such a small thing compared to my happiness. I had to decide what I was willing to put up with and I had made my decisions because I was happy. I had pushed away the people closest to me, later on realizing these were all his intentions. The only people I talked to were the people in his family and a few close friends. At the time, that seemed like enough for me, but he set up life in a way where I had no freedom and depended on him for everything.

betrayal

and

disloyalty

CHAPTER FOUR

Lies and More Lies

Things started to take a turn when our baby girl was born. At this time, he had three phones, which he said he used for his "car business". He told me that he went in fifty-fifty with his friend to buy a McLaren to rent out because they wanted to start an exotic car rental business together. Starting a business like this meant that they would be gone a lot of days and nights to drop the car off for the people who wanted to rent it.

What went from him spending every waking day with me, had started turning into him leaving several nights a week for this business he told me about. I was home with the kids and trying to get in my new routine of having a newborn again, while he was gone for several days of the week. He was very secretive with his phones as well. Who uses three phones? I distinctly remember one night, I woke up at 2:00 a.m. worrying about what happened to him, and he still wasn't home. I kept calling, but the calls kept going to voicemail. He finally got home after 4:00 a.m. and he told me that after he dropped the car off to the person, he didn't have service and he got sick and had to pull over on the side of the road, which is why it took him so long to get home.

I just knew something was off, but I chose to ignore my gut feeling. There was one day we got into an argument because all of a sudden, he told me he wanted to see his friends and I kept

Chapter Four

complaining because in the two years we were together, this was never an issue for him. I'll say that again, he wanted to see his "friends". He never had this behavior before our baby was born, but all of a sudden it was like he never wanted to be home.

He also told me our landlord had a friend who was the main person that did Ted X and they wanted him to come and travel to speak about his experience trading since he was so successful. One day, he was gone the entire day and told me they were having a meet-up at this guy's house and there were several people there that the guy was interested in doing Ted X with. Another night, he met this guy for dinner, but the funny thing is, he stayed out until after the restaurant closed. When I questioned him about this, he said the guy hadn't finished speaking to him, so they proceeded to talk by his car for another two hours. How idiotic I was back then to even believe someone would have so much to talk about, that they would have to take the conversation to their car for hours.

How foolish could I have been to believe this nonsense? He said the guy wanted to pay him over 2 million dollars to do Ted X and he was doing this to get more income. This is a story that would soon disappear and he would blame it on not wanting to travel and leave me behind because I was questioning what he was doing late at night. How convenient. He met with this "guy" and talked to him so much. He even said he had to meet the guy late at night to get the initial check for him to do Ted X. He said he deposited the check a few days later, but never showed me proof of it. Shortly after that, he decided not to move forward with the business deal because he was so concerned about how I would feel about him traveling. It caught me off guard when he said he wasn't moving forward because he had previously told me that the two-million-dollar check had already been deposited in his account.

Around June 2023, when baby girl was already a few weeks old, we were playing video games upstairs. My phone lit up when he was next to me, and I received an anonymous message on

Facebook saying "No one wanted to tell you, but I think you deserve to know". His picture was posted in a group because he was seeing other women and they wanted to see if he was married. At that exact moment, my heart dropped and my head started to spin. The man who I spent the last two and a half years with, the man who I thought was my other half, was now standing in a picture hugging another woman. It was at this exact moment that my life would forever be changed.

My kids were already sleeping in bed, and here I was helpless, getting a random message from a stranger who possibly could have saved my life and future. I showed him the message. Now some people say a psychopath shows no emotions when confronted because they don't process things like other people do. When he looked at the message, he immediately answered, oh someone said the same thing about you and people are just trying to get us down because they can't stand us being happy. What stood out about this picture that was posted online, referring to my then fiancé as "Ryan Gallo", was that his beard was gray and the hat he was wearing was recently purchased. I even brought that up to him and he had nothing to say except they were lying. That night, I had a feeling in the pit of my stomach that something wasn't right, but it wasn't the time to go digging into it. If he said he would never cheat on me, then I was going to believe him. I mean what kind of monster would do that after they saw how much pain their fiancé went through to have their baby a few weeks ago? I guess you could say it's the same type of monster that would let a person who just went through over 30 hours of labor, practically sleep on the floor right after having a baby.

About two days after that initial confrontation, I decided to join the group myself and post anonymously asking if anyone had been on a date with him. Something just kept eating away at me and I had to get to the bottom of it. It took a little while for anyone to respond acknowledging dealing with him directly, but

Chapter Four

I got responses such as "he's been posted a lot lately" and he goes by such and such. Then finally, the one message I had been waiting for, was in my inbox. It was a girl who messaged me and said she didn't want to say anything but wanted to confront me in hopes that she could prevent this from happening to anyone else.

Since he had left the house to pick my son up the day I got the message, I took the opportunity to call her. She started telling me things that made my head spin. He went by the name Ryan Gallo and he had an entirely separate social media account. He was living a completely separate life. How could someone do this knowing they were engaged and had an entire family at home? It wasn't just a normal family either, it was a supportive and loving family. She told me that he would drive an hour away to pick her up and then he would take her out on dates all night. I found out he took her to Disney after Dark and the very next week took me there as well. He would find excuses to make grocery store trips just so he could talk to her on the phone the entire time in privacy. During this time, his grandfather passed away and I even found out he had a date lined up with her the day of the funeral. It all made sense. He was always outside on the phone circling our pool so I couldn't hear his conversations and he would simply tell me he was on business calls. This girl would be the first of many that came forward about his cheating.

Before his grandfather passed away in July 2023, I wanted to be present at the hospital every day that he was there, which was about a week. I did everything in my power to be supportive, because truly, his grandfather meant a lot to me. I was there for the funeral, I was there for all of it. I spent over five hundred dollars buying a basket of eighty-six white roses to represent his age and to try to bring the family some sort of comfort and peace. I bought each of the grandfathers' daughters a heart necklace that had a heart inside of it, to represent that a piece of him was always with them. All while this was happening, he was off in his world, becoming more and more distant, and stopped being the man I had known for the past few years. Then again, I don't think I ever really knew who this man was. I was trying to be caring and as sympathetic as possible during this tragic time, meanwhile, he was out talking to every girl that would give him attention.

Again, the word monster is all that comes to my head. On the day of the funeral, he dropped me and the baby off at home and showed up in his "business rental" McLaren to meet his family, and even went to the length of telling them that he had to drop the car off for a customer for his so-called car business. These were some of the many excuses he used to go out and cheat. On the days that I would get upset because all he wanted to do was hang out with his "friends", he would call me crazy and tell me I needed to trust him. There was one day when he canceled plans with the person he was cheating on me with because I got upset. I found out that he told her that he had to cancel their plans because he was in the hospital and had been in a horrible car accident. I'm not sure if the cheating part was worse or if how he went about doing it was worse.

He used one of his three phones to create a fake Facebook account pretending to be a woman. Then, he would use this identity to find a woman to hook them up with the identity's "friend", which was him. He went on Bumble and lured women in thinking they were talking to a girl who had a friend and would try to set these girls up with the "friend". To clarify, because it takes a true mastermind to do this, he was both the friend and the girl. I'm not sure what type of psychopath could pull this off, but he seemed to do it very well.

I had gotten other comments on the post I made from his ex-girlfriends from several years ago telling me that he had always been a scammer and serial cheater. The more I dove into this entire cheating thing, the more I started uncovering who he really was as a person. When he was driving to Melbourne to cheat on me,

Chapter Four

he was telling everyone he was a big-shot real estate developer who sold properties to celebrities. His fake social media also reflected that lifestyle and had over twenty thousand followers.

In the days to come, I wanted to confront him about the cheating again. At first, I tried to play it off as if I knew nothing because I didn't know where my life was going to end up once the truth came to light. I kept thinking that I quit my job to have this false reality of life. I was completely maxed out in debt. I had no money to fall back on because he wasn't giving me anything. I had two kids to raise. Where was I supposed to go from here? The word helplessness was all I could think of when I tried to describe my feelings at that exact moment. When I simply couldn't handle the agony and pain anymore, I confronted him. He denied everything and made me seem as if I was the crazy one. He even shed tears saying he would never hurt me like this. Boy, was he a good actor and manipulator.

One night, I asked the girl he was cheating on me with, if I could call her and put her on speakerphone to confront him and prove to him that I knew he was lying. She agreed that it would be okay and as I did that, he STILL kept denying everything. He kept saying this was a girl he dated before me, and even while she was on speaker, he was telling her she was a liar. I remember her voice and her confronting him saying "Ryan, stop lying to her". He had no shame and no remorse for what he had done.

He even went to the extent of making a fake profile and sending himself a message pretending to be the person who initially posted him in the group accusing him of being a cheater. The extent only a true psychopath would take to cover his tracks. He told me that he was waiting for the right time to show me this message. When I read the message, right away, I knew it was a lie. The message claimed to be from a girl who was apologizing and she said she was so sorry for everything. The message went on to say a group of girls wanted to ruin his life and that's why they made a fake post about

Lies and More Lies

him cheating. It also said that they didn't think it would cause so much harm. In my head, I was thinking, if you wanted to go the length of making a post like this to ruin someone's life, how did you not know it would cause so much harm?

Two days after the speakerphone confrontation, he told me there was something he needed to sit down and tell me. It was at this moment that he FINALLY came clean about cheating, but only said it was with that one girl. He got caught and was still lying! Even though I already knew the truth, hearing him say those words made me bawl my eyes out. I don't know why I expected a different reaction or outcome.

What I will never understand is how someone could show the world on their actual social media how in love they were, and in the background make a fake profile and pretend to be someone completely different. I found out the Ryan Gallo profile was made the month we moved into the new house. What were the happiest moments of my life in 2022, was the start of his other identity. Everything that made me smile that year, turned out to be a reason I should've cried, because it was never real. The dozens of flowers he bought me throughout the years, were used as a ploy to hide the fact that he was betraying me in the background.

In the moments that I had to take care of my kids and process his cheating, I started sleeping in the apartment connected to the house. There were several nights where he would break down crying and pretend to be the victim and say things like he couldn't believe he would do this to our family, as if I was supposed to feel sorry for him. For days, as much as I tried to hide how broken I was, my son watched me cry my eyes out and told me almost daily, "Mom, you deserve better than this." My eight-year-old son was trying to console me, while this grown man was still going behind my back and cheating on me. What's even worse is that while he was cheating and texting other girls when he was sitting next to me on the couch, my mind was focused on planning our wedding.

Chapter Four

There were days when I went wedding dress shopping and I had already sent our save the dates out, all while he was texting girls and finding excuses to run to Publix, just so he could talk to them on the phone. I remember the feeling when I found my dream wedding dress and pictured what it would be like to walk down the aisle to the song I had chosen. Even just the thought of it would make me cry because I was so happy that I was getting to marry the person who I thought was the man of my dreams. I cried so many times picturing that moment, just out of pure joy. I would even cry in the car when the song came on, simply because my heart felt so happy.

After everything started unraveling, I could picture the wedding, but instead of walking down the aisle, it was like someone wrapped their hands around me and they were pulling me away from him because this wedding was never going to happen. What I had been counting down months for, turned into something that would never happen. The same dresses that made me cry and feel like a princess, I would eventually have to sell. One person took all of the happiness inside of me and completely shattered every part of my heart. One person used my trust against me and took it for granted.

arrogance

and

deceit

CHAPTER FIVE
When Does It End?

There was a time when my little girl was a few weeks old before I found out about all of the cheating and we had decided to take a family trip to Key West. We were all supposed to be flying on a private jet, but the night before this was supposed to happen, he said the pilot got COVID so we ended up getting a "luxurious" sprinter van from the "Lamborghini" dealership. Well, that's what he said anyway. On the way to Key West, he kept saying how much he loved me and his entire family was in awe. His sister even made a comment to her husband asking why he never said these cute little things to her. During the ride there, he said he had made us all thousands of dollars by putting in a trade. What more could someone possibly ask for? Being loved in front of the entire family, having my girl next to me and my son sitting across from me, all while making money? What a dream.

I found out about his cheating two months after our trip to Key West. One day, after he swore he would never cheat again, I walked into our room, the room that used to be our safe space and was no longer familiar to me. I saw him texting on the phone and I asked him to see what he was writing because I could tell it was a paragraph. He immediately turned off his phone and kept making up lies. What a shock. He said he would never cheat on me again, yet he couldn't come clean about the paragraph he was

Chapter Five

sending to someone. He immediately went to the bathroom and erased all of the evidence. After he came out of the bathroom, he handed his phone to me, thinking everything that I shouldn't see had been erased. He proceeded to tell me that he had nothing to hide and that I could freely look through his phone. I found some disturbing stuff on there because he didn't completely delete everything. This in itself was enough for me to call it quits. As always, he kept making up excuses, saying he never searched for what I found, it just popped up and he clicked on it. As if everything else wasn't enough, this was more for me to process and try to be "normal" about the situation I was going through. During the next few weeks, we were on a rocky road and it felt like this phase of my life was never going to end. Little did I know what was in store for me and the kids was far worse than what I had already uncovered.

When I told him I was finished with his lies, he left to go to his parents' house because he needed to get away. During the entire time he was there, he kept texting me and I refused to respond, until he sent me a text saying "911". I immediately called him, because I wasn't completely heartless and wanted to know what had happened. I would later find out that he sent that message because I was ignoring his other messages, and he wanted to get my attention.

When I called him to find out what had happened, he was sobbing and told me that he had gotten in a car accident because he left his parents' house to pick up a car from his second garage, and someone hit him. He proceeded to pretend that he was talking to the police officer and the person who hit him, saying he was getting his license and registration. He even went as far as telling me that he thought his leg was broken, and later came home limping that night. While this incident was happening, I texted his sister, who in turn called her father. His dad said he could see him across the street in the car he showed up in, and he was just

When Does It End?

parked there. The accident that he described to me so well, was non-existent and in fact, nothing close to that even happened. I guess he forgot his location was still on, and I could see that he was near his parents' house. The fake accident was just another one of his psychopathic lies.

After this happened, I played it off as if he actually got in an accident, because I still needed to stay one step ahead of him to figure my life out. I had to make him believe that I knew nothing, and I was willing to give him another chance. This was secretly my way of trying to buy time to get out of this broken relationship. I even took it as far as agreeing to go to therapy with him.

During the initial therapy session, the therapist sat down with us and he admitted we were there because of his cheating. The first session was good, but I couldn't get past what he had done. We went to another session, but this time it was just me. She wanted to make sure I was safe with the kids and in the home we were living in. As I started telling her what was really going on and the lies he was feeding me, I'll never forget the look she had on her face. There was even a moment where she had to pause because she said she was trying to take everything in and process it. Imagine, a therapist couldn't process what was going on in my life, think of how I was supposed to process it as the person to whom it was happening to.

After what I told her, she made it clear that he needed extensive therapy to just be semi-normal. She told me the lies he told me weren't what a normal person did. I specifically remember her hearing about the fake car accident and saying "Look at what he's telling you, look at what he's doing for attention". She was absolutely right. He wasn't able to control his lies and those lies eventually became his reality. Seeing as he's taken money from people for several years, I doubt he had any intention of stopping anytime soon. While the truths were unraveling, he kept blaming me for everything that was coming out into the open. He said if

Chapter Five

I didn't open my mouth, even if I was speaking the truth, then none of this would have happened. I had spoken to several people in his family since he had also taken money from them. They told me they had always known him to be a scammer and didn't warn me because they saw how happy he was, and thought he had truly changed for the better. It just turned out that he was better at hiding his scams because we had a life together and were building a family together, something he never had before.

As more lies continued to unfold, I wanted to always stay one step ahead of him so I wouldn't end up on the street with my children. I called my friend whose daughter was pregnant at the time, and told her to come pick some stuff up from me that she could use for the baby. I waited until he was gone that day so she could come to the house and he wouldn't suspect what I was doing. He was always watching the ring cameras outside when he wasn't home because he always wanted to keep tabs on me. I didn't know how I was going to get money or have a future for my kids, so I told my friend to come over and when she did, I put all of my designer bags in trash bags and put them in storage containers. I had begun moving stuff out of the house before he could take them and sell them himself. I made the excuse up that my friend was coming over to pick up baby clothes, as our daughter had already outgrown them. He didn't question this and although he immediately noticed my designer bags were missing, I said I simply put them in a safe place so nothing else would go missing from the house. I was already missing a diamond bracelet worth over eight thousand dollars that he bought me on Valentine's Day, as well as my Gucci pajamas worth over five thousand dollars, which I knew he undoubtedly took.

I also thought to myself that I needed a backup way to contact people in case he canceled my phone plan if he ever found out I knew as much as I did. I was thinking that going through all these hoops was something you'd see straight out of a Lifetime Movie, because in all honesty, who has to do this? I went through my belongings and found an old phone of mine and I had to make a fake number on it, just in case of an "emergency". I'll never forget the day I sat on the bathroom floor with the door locked. He wasn't home yet, but he could've shown up at any given moment and I was terrified, to the point where my hands were shaking while I was adding in contacts. I managed to get the new number working and I ran upstairs and hid the phone in a place he would never think to look. I had only given close people this number because they already knew what had been going on. As funny as it was, his mother was one of the people who had my emergency number. Go figure. The same person who turned their back on me as soon as their family name was in jeopardy.

beware,

caution

CHAPTER SIX
Can't Run from the Truth

I began talking to his sister after I found the disturbing stuff on his phone that wanted me to run far far away. It turns out that both siblings share the same issue when it comes to being pathological liars. I don't know if it stems from wanting and craving attention, or if it has something to do with genetics, but something was off with both siblings. When I say she's a liar, she is the type that just takes a story and changes it to make it more extreme and make it more dramatic to get attention for herself.

When we first moved into the house, his mom was there spending the weekend with us and we were in the hot tub just talking and spending quality time with each other. All of our phones were inside the house because we didn't think we needed them since we planned on being in the hot tub. His sister kept trying to call all of us and when we didn't answer, she called the cops and told them she thought we may have been murdered or something. The cops showed up and laughed and left after they realized nothing was wrong. I also found out that when we didn't answer our phones, she called her dad, who was in Vegas at the time, and said what if one of her brother's scams caught up to him and someone came to the house for that reason to kill us. It's like they knew about his scamming all along and let him get away with it. Even though both siblings lied uncontrollably, I got enough

Chapter Six

information from her that I could verify with their parents as well, and that's when the truth started coming out about everything, more than I had already found out.

It got to the point where his sister was texting me every day and we were going back and forth with the information we knew. I called her each time he left the house and we talked about his lies and his past and we were able to uncover so many different things about him. That alone can paint a picture of how long this guy has been scamming people. He's a bit worse with his lies because he will lie about any and everything, just to get by in life.

Luckily, while I started uncovering his lies, my mother was in town to provide the emotional support I needed. I have a very small circle of support and in front of his face I had to act like I knew nothing, whereas, in reality, I knew everything I needed to. I found out that his lies started from the very first day that I met him. Remember how I said he was leasing a house and the reason I was never able to go over there was because he told me he had boxes everywhere? The real reason he didn't want me visiting his home and came to me every day instead, was because he was still living at home with his parents! When he met me online, it was the perfect opportunity for him to sweet talk me and use me, knowing that I was about to have my own home and it would be a way for him to move out of his parents' house and into mine.

He previously told me that he was married and he was evicted from his apartment because he wasn't in love with the person he was married to at the time. He said he left her there at the apartment and moved back in with his parents. Eventually, there was an eviction notice because she stopped paying for the apartment. How can a person pay for an apartment when they were promised that they could stay at home and not have to work? This all sounded too familiar. The truth to that story was he stopped paying for no reason at all, and they both moved back to his parents' house, until one day her parents came and picked her up because he was treating her like trash. I even heard that he would leave her at his parents' house and go out all day, and sometimes all he would get her to eat was a can of tuna. The person I knew, was a completely different man than the one I was planning on saying "I Do" to.

I also found out that at the very beginning of our relationship, as an excuse for me not to go to his nonexistent "home", he told little lies saying his sister was staying with him for weeks at a time because she got in a fight with her husband, and he didn't want me over there. He told me he graduated from the University of Central Florida with a Bachelor's degree, truth be told, he dropped out of high school with no degree in sight. This house he told me he had in Mexico, was non-existent. The Kia he had when we first met that he said he bought for his ex-wife, turned out to be HIS car all along, as confirmed by his parents. He told me he had a lot of real estate properties, again, another lie. He even lied to the point where he said he used to have abs and it turned out that he used Photoshop to make fake abs for the world to see. What kind of human being lies about the littlest things, like how you got marks on your back? What kind of person is so desperate for attention that they keep their lies going for several years, without realizing how it affects every single person around you?

I remember being upstairs while he was away on one of his dates, and I started diving into all of my credit card statements. He was an authorized user on one of my cards because I wanted to help him build his credit. I started seeing charges from places like Gucci, Louis Vuitton, and International Diamond Center. He even charged my card for seven thousand dollars to let his friends stay at the Penthouse at the Wave Hotel and then played it off like he was the one paying for everything. As I started seeing all of these charges, I realized, he wasn't buying all of these luxurious gifts for me, I was buying my own presents with my credit card! He even put a six-thousand-dollar charge to the car rental company.

Chapter Six

A company that I had no idea existed at the time because he told me he was buying all of these cars. When he put the charge on my card, he said the charge was made to Lamborghini and had to be done because it was the very last payment he owed to own the Lamborghini Urus. A few weeks after that charge, he said that the car kept shutting off and it had to be fixed. Lo and behold, after it was sent in to be "repaired", I never saw the car again. I still have no idea why that much was charged to my card for a rental car, but I know that he used me and put me in more debt because of it.

This leads me to the time when I was driving around in the Lamborghini Urus and I started to question why he never gave me a physical insurance card, and also why I didn't have a registration, since he claimed he bought the car for me. He played it off and kept saying he would take care of it later. After hearing this for months, I told him this wasn't okay because if I got pulled over, I would get in trouble. He sat on the computer for a few minutes and printed out this piece of paper that looked as if a kindergartner had copied and pasted words and images onto a sheet of paper. When I asked what the paper in front of me was, he said it was all the information I needed for the car. Keep in mind, that this paper was not an actual insurance card and he even spelled his last name wrong on this fake document he created and claimed was an insurance card.

He proceeded to tell me that all the police would have to do if they pulled me over was look up my license plate and they would find all the information they needed. I worked for an insurance company for 9 years, so I wasn't going to let that false statement go. I had to go run errands that day and I called him and told him by the time I got home I needed to see proof of actual insurance because it wasn't okay to let me drive around with no insurance. When I arrived home, he gave me an entirely new insurance card that listed a different company than before, in which the effective date was that same day. At this moment, I knew I had been driving around for several months with absolutely no insurance.

Shortly after this, I started receiving mail saying my coverage was going to end because the payment he made for that insurance had bounced, so he still owed the company the full amount. I kept telling him he needed to pay and every single time, he would respond telling me he paid it. I started receiving letters saying they were going to send me to collections because the insurance was under my name and they still weren't getting payment for my insurance. The only way I was able to resolve the issue was to contact the insurance company myself and explain that I never actually owned that car, and my ex was a scam artist.

There was a day where I questioned whether my hundred-thousand-dollar engagement ring was real or not so I had to set up a plan. I went to the mall and had my friend meet me there. I went into two jewelry stores at the mall so they could diamond test my ring. The two people looked at me in disbelief when I said I was told it was a real genuine diamond. They had confirmed it was not. Finally, I decided to leave my phone with my friend and I took her phone with me and went to the actual store where he bought the ring. I had to take these measures because my location was on and he could see exactly where I was, and I knew he was always watching. At the store he bought the band from, they were able to pull up his account and told me that the "real" diamond he bragged to everyone about getting me, was a lab-made diamond, not a genuine diamond, and it wasn't worth half of what he said it was. From what I've mentioned earlier, it isn't about material things. I care more about someone lying to me, telling my family that the ring on my finger could buy a house, whereas, in reality, it couldn't even buy a piece of land.

Another time, he told me he was going to my bank to deposit money so I could use that to make my minimum credit card payments. From what he told me he was going to deposit and

Chapter Six

what he actually deposited, I was short by about two thousand dollars. When I confronted him about it, he kept telling me the bank made a mistake and I needed to contact them and tell them to do an audit because this was entirely their fault. Later on, he admitted that he shorted me on purpose because he forgot he had a bill to pay and that was the only money he had to use to pay it.

His exes from the past, even ten years before our relationship had reached out to me and told me that he had another kid with someone over ten years ago. The last time he saw his daughter was when she was little and in a car seat. He denied ever having this baby to his family and abandoned her. What a heartless human being.

He even lied about small things, like saying he never took people to the places we took trips to. On the trips we went on, he told me he always wanted to take a woman there with him because it was so romantic, but never had the right person. Turns out he had already taken someone else to the same places we went to, years before meeting me, even down to the ice-skating place in Utah, and there were even pictures to prove it. Who was this man? This was not the person I sat down at the bar with in 2021 talking to all night until the bar closed. The person I felt like I could see a future with. The person that I had been planning my future with.

I kid you not, every other week he would come up with several stories about how he was going to pay off my debt. He even took it as far as saying he spoke to the manager at the bank, and they agreed to get the Brinks truck to bring a million dollars in cash because that's how much he claimed to have in his account. He said I would have to go with him as well as his dad because all that money would be very heavy for us to carry. He also said he was ordering safes for the house because we needed somewhere to store the money after it was picked up. I found it rather fishy that the safes never arrived, and as you can guess, there was a reason why we weren't able to pick up the money from the bank. He's told many stories to a lot of different people, but the story that he had been holding onto the longest was that the IRS froze all of his accounts because his accountant took 1.5 million dollars that he was supposed to use to pay his taxes back in 2023, and kept it for himself. He said that the IRS was doing an investigation with the accountant, but in the meantime, he had no access to any of his accounts.

This was all too convenient because it was his reason for not giving people "profit" from their trading accounts when they asked for it. As he was telling one person his accounts were frozen, he was telling other people who didn't know about the situation, that he was trading for them during that entire time. He would send fake screenshots showing that he made thousands of dollars from his trades, and sometimes didn't catch on to the fact that the dates on the screenshots didn't match the timeline that he was telling them he was doing trades. He became a professional when it came to saying "The wire will be here next week". How many times can a person hear that for two years? I guess it was only his accounts that had issues, and the banks only messed up wires and transfers for him and no one else.

As time went on, I was trying to handle the stress the best I could. I simply didn't know where to go from there. I had given up my life's work because I put my trust in someone else's hand, and it was clear that all he was good at, was lying, to try to cover his tracks. I started to become smarter and find ways to protect myself and do what I needed to to get out of this situation. I reached out to our landlord, who immediately told me that he was getting suspicious already because he had been asking for some of his profit months before I called, and there was always a reason not to give it to him. I told him the same thing was happening to me. The sad part is that he had taken money from everyone he could think of, including his family members. He even told his brother-in-law to quit his job. He said he could invest with him

Chapter Six

and he would have an incoming salary solely from the profit he was making for him. He paid him for about two months, and after that, the brother-in-law no longer had an income.

Regardless of all of the evidence and information I was finding out, he always reassured me that he was going to pay off my credit card debt. He even said if we weren't together, he was going to give me enough money so I could afford to get a car and a house to care for the kids. He told me I would have enough money to continue being a stay-at-home mom. I don't know what was going through my head because I was semi-hopeful that this would happen. He was making calls to car dealerships and telling them to hold the car that I liked, and truly acting as if he was buying me a car. I saw the messages and I even called the dealership myself and that's when I realized it was another one of his lies.

After days had gone by of his false promises of trying to get me a car, he started telling me stories like the car sold and they weren't getting new cars that I liked any time soon. After talking to the guy at the dealership who worked with him directly, he told me that the only thing preventing me from getting the car was that they were waiting for him to send the wire. Oh, another fake wire. I don't think I need to tell you that I'm still waiting for the money for the house, for a car, and to pay off my debt. He can't even afford to send money for me to get groceries or diapers for our daughter, much less for everything else.

bitterness and resentment

CHAPTER SEVEN
Victims

I was lying in bed one day and I received a text from a random number asking if it was me. My heart started beating very fast because I could only imagine what this person had to tell me, after everything I had already found out. She finally responded the day after. She said she had been a friend of his for years before my relationship with him. They had worked together at a theme park and she went on to explain that during COVID, her father had passed away and left her an inheritance of over one hundred thousand dollars. When my relationship began with him, I had no idea that he was texting her saying he had heart issues and needed surgery. Being the good friend that she was, and knowing nothing about his scamming, she gave him the money for his so-called surgery. He even went to the extent of pretending to be me and texting people saying that he was healing well and how grateful he was to have the money for the surgery. He not only stole her money for a fake surgery but also used my identity to thank people.

In the months following his fake heart surgery, this victim told me that he continued his lies saying he had an Airbnb and in order for her to get her money back, she would have to send thousands of dollars to his account and she would get the money back and more when it was refunded. When that situation happened, Airbnb locked her account and all of the money was released to him. There were times when he tried paying off all of my credit card debt and it would go through for about a week and then bounce back. After I told her about that, she looked at her bank statements, and it showed that he was using her bank account number to try to pay off all of my credit cards.

The payments were going to bounce back because it was fraudulent activity, and he knew this but he used it to buy him more time. He did this to get me off his back for a few days and make me think my cards were going to be paid off. The amount of money he was trying to move from her bank to pay off my cards was over sixty thousand dollars. The banks kicked back the payments because she didn't have that kind of money in her account. With her alone, he stole over one hundred thousand dollars. The money that was supposed to be left to her during a sad time, became money that was a part of his scheme. It all made sense when she gave him money for his fake heart surgery, that was the same time frame that he showed up at my home with the McLaren. While he was planning fancy trips for him and me, he was texting her saying he needed money for hospital bills and she would give it to him. She was funding his luxurious lifestyle with me and had no idea.

What makes me sad is his family was always supportive of our relationship. They thought there was no one better for him, other than me. Even his mother told me after she found out he cheated that if he could choose anyone it would be me. That's such a funny statement to me, seeing as he cheated and didn't choose me, instead, he did the complete opposite.

As the truth started to come out, I maintained a relationship with them and I continued telling them what I was finding out. In the beginning, they were supportive and tried to be a listening ear the best they could. As things progressed quickly and got worse, I will never forget their words, "We love you, but he will always be our son". Those words itself reminded me that I was alone in this

Victims

situation, and no matter how much damage he did, they would always be on his side to cover for him, which is exactly what they did. I heard all the crazy stories that were being made up about me. Funny how one day you're in the circle, and the next day you're a complete stranger. The things that were being said about me, now that the truth was finally out, were beyond belief and the best word to describe it was unimaginable. Some say blood is thicker than water, and I would have to agree with that statement in my situation.

I couldn't imagine the feeling of raising a child who is a scammer and gets enjoyment out of using everyone else's hard-earned money. A child that lies about the smallest things in life and starts believing all of those lies are true, simply because he was so used to lying. When I confronted his family about his fake car accident, I was told "Oh he's only doing that for attention", and they blew it off like it was no big deal. How could you even support such a monster? How could you turn against the one person who was there through everything and blame her for your son acting this way? How could you turn your back on the mother of your grandchild and not show any type of support, yet claim you love your grandchild more than life itself?

It's always easy to point the finger at someone else, instead of acknowledging that you indeed, created a monster and you are the ones to blame for him being like this. Every single time they found out he was in trouble and scammed people in the past, they took him back in, simply because it was "their son". I just don't understand how someone could repeatedly do this to several people and get away with it. Then again, look at everything else that was happening in my life, I should have expected nothing different.

One by one, I was coming in contact with all of the people he had scammed and taken money from. I came in contact with another one of his "friends" that he worked at a different theme

Chapter Seven

park with, who he also took money from. This time, the reason was to invest in a home in Mexico for an Airbnb. This guy had known him for many years and had just lost his job, so he saw this as an opportunity to make money. He gave him money that was never repaid to him. The building he wanted to invest in, was another scam of his. His friend had been to Mexico with him and was watching him make money while doing foreign exchange trading. Doesn't it sound appealing? You get to sit on the beach in Mexico, enjoy food, enjoy the company, and make money while you're barely doing anything. If it seems too good to be true, it's simply because it is.

Another person reached out to me during this time, saying she worked for a luxury rental car company. Now, this is what hit me hard and made me realize what a liar and scammer he was. This person even drove past our house when she was owed money, and instead of paying her back, he kept threatening her. Who threatens someone THEY owe money to? I guess the answer to that question would be someone who doesn't have the money to pay that person back, so he tried to scare them instead.

It turned out all of these luxury cars he claimed to own, were simply all rentals. Every single one of them. I had no idea. He told me he had a whole separate garage because all of the cars wouldn't fit in our home garage. Another lie. She told me she knew about me from the start of our relationship. She was one of the first people to even find out I was pregnant. She said for the gender reveal he was very adamant about having three exotic cars there. From what I now know about him, he wanted those cars there to show off in front of our family and friends. Why else would someone spend thousands and thousands of dollars to have three cars at a house for people to stare at? Even back at that time, he didn't pay her for the cars to be at the gender reveal, so she let him borrow the cars and she used money out of her own pocket, which has yet to be repaid. She thought she was doing a friend a favor since he had already done a ton of business with their company. She even confirmed that the year before, he spent hundreds and thousands of dollars just renting cars. My guess is after they had a falling out, he found a new company to rent cars from and tried moving on without having to pay her back. He had never owned any of the cars he claimed he did. He lied to the world about this fake garage and all these cars that were his. Why would someone do that? To lure people in to make them think that he was making a ton of money, so they could approach and do business with him. To date, she still has not been paid what was owed to her.

Another situation involved a guy who owned an art class. We had been there several times and he always treated us well. Well, one day he decided to ask if his money could be invested. He of course saw all of the cars that were being driven and followed him on social media, so again, who wouldn't want a piece of the pie? He decided to give him a few thousand dollars to invest and when he asked for his money back, he only got a portion of it. This person had personally reached out to me, and I had no idea what the situation was, so I simply said I didn't want to get involved. I had no idea that this exact situation would be something I would be dealing with a few months later.

I never got involved with any of his investments and what he was doing for other people, simply because he told me he was making me money and I knew he was getting good business. What I didn't know was that most of these people weren't getting their money back, and when they asked, there was always some excuse as to why. When he would get angry at people for asking for money back, whether it was profit or money from their original investment, he would text them and threaten them and find ways to talk negatively about them as a person. How could you try to make someone question their character when they did nothing wrong? He had so many reasons why he couldn't send people their profit. On some days he would say the trades weren't doing well, other days he would say the banks were having issues, wires weren't going through, and so on.

I watched a movie on Netflix called Anna Delvey, and if this doesn't remind you of it, then I don't know what does. I told him he was the male version of Anna Delvey because that is exactly who he was and continues to be. He wasn't fond of the comments I made and continued to blame me for everything, but I swore to myself I was never going to stop telling the truth. I told him I wasn't a liar like he was and if someone approached me about what I knew, I was going to say everything I knew.

Yet again, there was another woman I found who he took money from. It's almost as if he targeted women with children that he met on dating apps because he sees them as weak. This one particular woman told me it started as flirting and she sent me all of their messages from the start of their interaction to the finish. When it finally came time for them to meet up, it was strictly about "investing". Another victim. He took money from her and when she kept asking for it back, he started to become condescending towards her. He used her weaknesses to throw them back in her face. He would make comments like "No wonder your husband cheated on you, look at you". This all seemed too familiar. From my personal experience with him, after I wouldn't take him back after cheating, he made similar comments to me saying "No wonder I cheated on you, you're garbage, the worst piece of trash", and so on. She eventually found out he was engaged and I was pregnant and I think she was one of the only people who got her money back from him because she kept threatening to tell on him.

What jars my mind is before all of this came out into the open, his family came to our house and the day before we had watched the Tinder Swindler on Netflix. Well, he liked this movie so much that he suggested putting it on so his family could watch it, which meant that we would also rewatch it. The funny thing is, as we were watching it and being entertained, we had no idea this was

Victims

exactly what he was doing to every one of us. Looking back, this takes a special type of psychotic person to do this. I also found out he made a fake GoFundMe several months after his grandfather had passed away. His GoFundMe said that his grandfather was beaten by a bunch of men and was on life support. He even took it far enough to use a photo of when his grandfather was in the hospital bed. Seeing as he had a date lined up for the day of his grandfathers' funeral, this showed how emotionally disconnected he was, and was just desperate to scam others for money.

After the passing of his grandfather, he willingly met with members of the family, to tell them that he was eager to take the inheritance that the grandfather left to the grandkids and turn it into more money as it would be beneficial for the grandkids. At that moment, his scams were still in play, so who wouldn't want to give up a few thousand dollars and wait a few months to make way more money? With his false promises, he willingly took that inheritance money and to date, he hasn't paid a single penny back to the grandkids. As if we expected anything different to happen, knowing what we now know.

He started getting letters in the mail saying he owed money to everyone that you could possibly imagine. He was in debt to SeaWorld, to the place he bought his 200 gallon saltwater fish tank from, to the car rental companies, and to just about every place he used to make it look like he lived this large and extravagant life. Life was quickly spiraling down for him. It was spiraling down for me as well, because what was I supposed to do with no money and no job?

resilience, hope, transformation, healing

CHAPTER EIGHT
Facing Reality

Fast forward to what I'm dealing with today, let's just say some things never change. I was forced to sell all of my designer things and everything I could find that was worth a penny in the home we lived in together. When more details of his scams started to unfold, he would disappear for weeks at a time. At this point, I had no car that I owned, I had no money in my account, and two kids to care for.

There was one day when I sat outside after the kids were already in bed. I made a GoFundMe. Never in a million years would I think I'd be asking people for support and help. I was always independent. I spent a lifetime building the life I had before I met this man. I made a GoFundMe describing my situation in detail. I sat there and read it over and over, debating if posting it was the right thing to do. It took me hours of staring at the GoFundMe page before I got the courage to finally post it on social media. I finally thought to myself, what more do I possibly have to lose? This man has already taken every single thing away from me.

I am not one to ask others for help, I have always been able to take care of myself, and here I was, so desperate and asking the world for help. After a few minutes of posting it to social media, the support started rolling in and the world started learning about

Chapter Eight

my situation. The situation no one ever thought was possible or would have ever happened, based on our previous happy, dreamlike posts on social media. My posts with all of our trips and happy wedding planning had turned into my worst nightmare. I cried my eyes out that night, a feeling I would never forget. Truthfully, I am happy I made that post, the support was overwhelming and just what I needed to get by and keep fighting this tough fight.

As a mother, you know you would do anything to make sure your kids are able to get by. I even went as far as selling the fish tank that he paid over twenty thousand dollars for, for next to nothing, and selling the dining room furniture and bedroom furniture. I had to figure out where I was going to live, how I was going to get my son to school, how I was going to do anything. I counted on one person for everything, and in turn, he took everything away from me. We were already almost evicted from our home twice due to him not paying the rent on time. There were two separate occasions when he was gone and I was home with the kids, and the water was turned off one time and then the power was turned off another, due to lack of payment. I talked to our landlord, who had already reached his breaking point with him as well. He had invested a quarter of a million dollars and he wasn't getting any of his investment back, and rent was being paid late almost monthly now. I found out we had to be out of the house by March 1, 2024, which only gave me a few weeks to get my life together and completely start over.

For much of the last weeks left in February, he was gone, nonexistent. He would get up and leave the house and not tell me when he was going to be back. Sometimes he would be gone for weeks at a time. How could I possibly do this? How could I get my son ready for school, care for my daughter, and figure out our future that was supposed to start over in a few weeks? I remember one of the times he was gone, he said he was right down the street, and if I needed anything he would send it to me. My little girl had gotten sick, so I simply asked for medicine. He never sent it. I had hit rock bottom even more.

A few days after that, I was lying on the bottom bunk of my sons' bed when I got a random email from a girl who had seen my GoFundMe, and she asked me to contact her. This was 11:00 p.m. at night and my heart started racing. I spoke to her on WhatsApp and even though he said he was right down the street, I found out he had been in Mexico. He joined Bumble there and was taking a bunch of girls out on dates. He had money to stay at an Airbnb, but he didn't have any money to spare for the daughter he claims to care so much about or give us money for groceries. The girl told me she had seen him three times that past week and he was even going to her home and was paying for them to go out on dates.

Within a few days of meeting this stranger off the internet, they were diving into certain topics to get to know each other. He specifically told her he had no children and he owned a vacation rental in Florida. That same rental he told her about was the same home we shared together that we were being evicted from. He also said that he owned several Lamborghinis and was a successful Forex trader. If that didn't scream he was reeling her in to be his next victim, I don't know what does. I confronted him about his lies about being "down the street from our home", he simply told me to back off and mind my business. How could I mind my business when he wasn't providing for the child we had together? She was such a little innocent baby, but instead, he chose to provide for several women he had only known for a few hours.

In my head, I no longer cared about what he was doing and who he was with, I just wanted the ability to take care of my kids and pay off my debt, which he was refusing to help with. I had to figure out my life in such a short time and pack up a six thousand square foot house on my own while caring for my two children. Luckily, I did have some help from family and friends and was able to do it all in a short amount of time. The emotions and frustration

Chapter Eight

that I felt during this time were unbearable. I didn't know how I was going to survive this, how was I going to be able to provide for my kids and make sure they stayed happy without knowing how much all of this was killing me on the inside? He was still gone this entire time.

All I wanted more than anything at this point was to move out and just start over. I figured after I was out of the old house, I could meet up with him at a mutual location to swap our daughter to share our time with her. Two days after moving into my new home, I received a phone call from him reciting my address and laughing, saying he knew exactly where I had moved to. He went on to patronize me and continued to be as delusional as ever, so I had to hang up the phone when I couldn't take it anymore. He thought I secretly had all this money stored away and he truly had no idea how much I struggled to even find a place for the kids and me to live in. He will never understand the nights I cried my eyes out, because he was never there to witness it, yet here he was telling me that I was doing just fine on my own. What a true narcissist.

He was still talking down to me even though he had caused a lifetime of damage, meanwhile, not offering any help or trying to pay off any of the debt he put me in. I was out a car, a home, my investment, and he offered nothing at all. Instead, I was continuously being fed more and more lies about when I would get my money. Before I moved out of the house, he told me I would never have to work again and he had 2.8 million dollars for me. While we were still together and I was keeping track of his trades, I was at 5.5 million dollars in profit. He told me to keep dreaming about getting any of that back. Then, that story turned into, "I lost it all in a bad trade and you're going to have to find a job to survive".

Currently, he is still putting me through hell and back. He hired an attorney, one would call him the attorney you hire when you want to stay out of jail. He has been telling me for almost two years now that I would be debt-free, yet, here I am still struggling and fighting and living off the money I made from selling things, not to mention still being sixty-three thousand dollars in debt. He thinks that since he sees his daughter once in every blue moon, it deems him a good father and he shouldn't have to pay me anything, not even child support. He told me that since we weren't together, I needed to find a job and find a way to care for my children. His exact words were, "When I'm with my daughter I will pay for her, and when she's with you, you need to pay to care for her".

My credit card payments are several months late. I can even say two years late at this point, and he hasn't given me money to make the minimum payments, yet he expects me to just get up and get a job and care for the kids. I still hear the stories almost weekly from him about how he is bringing me cash and sending me wires, but boy have I learned not to trust a word he says. Why bother asking about something, when you simply know this person craves the attention and drama, thus, leaving you with nothing in the end? The times I ask him to pick up our daughter, there is always an excuse in place as to why he can't or why he's late. How can any person find a job, when the other party is so unreliable to take care of their own child? When a person would rather travel to Mexico to take girls out, versus buying his sick daughter medicine, that speaks volumes.

The one thing that I do find comical, is throughout this story, there were many red flags and situations where I should have questioned who this man was. I also asked myself over and over "Imagine if I had done this or did that differently, then I wouldn't be dealing with what I'm going through today". Looking at his point of view, he is probably thinking, "Imagine if I didn't cheat", or maybe even "What if I never met this woman". If he didn't cheat and never got caught, his scamming of ten-plus years, as well as his traits of being a pathological liar probably wouldn't

Chapter Eight

even have come to light. If he never met me, he wouldn't have someone investigating his lies, finding out his scams, and fighting every day to bring it all to light. As I remind myself, everything happens for a reason, and I was the reason why he was exposed. I was meant to be in this situation to prevent this from happening to his future victims.

Even though this nightmare doesn't seem to be ending anytime soon, I will always continue fighting for my kids, because one person shouldn't get to be the entity that ruins us. That would give him too much power that he doesn't deserve. I will continue spreading my story because another person shouldn't have to deal with the same lies and betrayal. For one person to work so hard to have a decent life and have it taken away in a heartbeat because someone is so selfish, isn't okay. To him, it's just another person he can scam, but to us, this is our life. I am looking forward to that one day when my daughter is old enough, and she will read these exact words that I have written. She will understand the struggles that I have been through, and will always remember how much she is loved by me and the good people that surround her. I will raise her right and teach her how to run far away if she ever encounters a bad man because she should never have to endure any of this pain in her lifetime. I am waiting for that day.

ABOUT THE AUTHOR

I was born on a small island and moved to the United States when I was five years old. Having to move to America brought many struggles on its own. My family struggled to make a living here for a very long time, but I saw first-hand what it was like to have nothing and work your way up to something, even if it was the smallest something you could call your own. I had to go to five elementary schools because as soon as we settled down and I made friends, it was time to get up and move again.

Life was never consistent for me, but it also taught me to never take anything for granted. I knew I wanted to be more for myself and I was willing to work hard in order to get there. I put in a lot of work to finish my degrees and create opportunities for myself. I was highly motivated to be independent and never had to depend on another person for my success. My success is currently reflected by knowing that I am raising two beautiful children in which I cherish with all of my heart. Having to start over from scratch hasn't been effortless, but I also know nothing good in life comes easy. I will get back to where I was one day, but until then, I will hold on to my inspiration and share my story with the world.

www.ingramcontent.com/pod-product-compliance
Lightning Source LLC
Chambersburg PA
CBHW032212040426
42449CB00005B/553